Also by Jill Bialosky

POETRY
Subterranean
The End of Desire

ANTHOLOGY
Wanting a Child
(coedited with Helen Schulman)

FICTION
The Life Room
House Under Snow

Intruder

Intruder

poems

Jill Bialosky

ALFRED A. KNOPF *New York* 2008

THIS IS A BORZOI BOOK
PUBLISHED BY ALFRED A. KNOPF

Published in the United States by Alfred A. Knopf,
a division of Random House, Inc., New York, and in
Canada by Random House of Canada, Limited, Toronto.

www.aaknopf.com

Knopf, Borzoi Books, and the colophon are registered
trademarks of Random House, Inc.

Library of Congress Cataloging-in-Publication Data
Bialosky, Jill.
Intruder : poems / by Jill Bialosky.—1st ed.
p.   cm.
"This is a Borzoi book"—T.p. verso.
ISBN 978-0-307-26847-1
I. Title.
PS3552 I19158 2008
811'.54—dc22   2008015430

Manufactured in the United States of America
First Edition

For David and Lucas

But what's art but an intense life—if it be real?
—HENRY JAMES, *The Lesson of the Master*

Contents

Demon Lover   3

I.

The Seduction   7
The Figure   9
The Poet Contemplates the Nature of Reality   10
Music is Time   11
The Poet Contemplates the Nature of Motherhood   12
Rules of Contact   13
The Poet Contemplates Her Calling   15
Cathedral of Wonder   16
Myth of Creation   17
The Poet Contemplates the Intensity of Emotions   18

II.

Intimacies: Portrait of an Artist   21
    1. The Seeker   21
    2. Adjoining Rooms   22
    3. Slumber Party   23
    4. Saturday Night   24
    5. Family Vacation   25

III.

In Contemplation of the Husband 29
Anniversary 30
Intruder 31
Subterfuge 33
The End of Love 34

IV.

The Skiers 37

V.

The Poet Contemplates the Sunflowers 49
The Poet Discovers the Significance
     of the Old Manuscripts 50
The Poet Contemplates the Wilderness 52
The Beauty of the Clearing 53
The Poet Returns Home for the Holidays 55
The Dream 56

VI.

Linked by Preverbal Feelings 59
The Poet Confronts the Self 60
Dreaming of Two Worlds Co-Existing in Harmony 61
An Essay in Two Voices 62
The Listener 63
Touch-Me-Nots 64
Lift Your Head, Speak 65
Basic Human Need Form 66

VII.

Snow in April 71
The Surfers 73
The Dream Life of the Poet 75

Notes 77
Acknowledgments 79

Intruder

DEMON LOVER

Is it still snowing?

Yes, she said.

Will it go on?

It will blanket the earth, she said.

It will fall

Over the hidden valleys and seep

Into the bark of the trees.

It won't end, she said.

Will you stay with me?

I won't leave, she said.

I must go then, said the lover.

I

THE SEDUCTION

It was ablaze, the room in the apartment building
facing the back courtyard where the poet slept,
and she woke not to the sound of sirens
but to glass breaking, voices shouting, *Get out, get out,*
and in her half dream she thought they were pranksters,
boys on the loose, wreaking havoc
in the courtyard between the two buildings.
Get dressed, he said, rushing into the room,
Just in case, and both thought about their boy
asleep in his bed, hoping they didn't have to wake him—
he was afraid of fire.
They walked to the picture window,
she in her long T-shirt, her husband already dressed
(prepared for disaster), and watched the fire—
it had spread into the courtyard between the buildings
determined to find all the unknown
private spaces and corridors.
There were small barrels of fire
like bonfires made to keep warm.
The engines drew close, the ladder
stretched out to the sixth floor
where the blaze bled flames strangely quixotic
and the hoses went off with such force
the water punctured windows, ricocheted off brick,
and it was gorgeous, dazzling,
the orange and reds of such ruin.
Once the water met the flames
the fire transfigured into smoke so thick
they could no longer see the fire trucks, the ladder,
the darkness, only gray, gaseous, colorless, ethereal
matter—still in half-dream—
she thought it must have been her internal desires
gone askew, reincarnated into the fist

of a god warning her against her window,
or Michelangelo's hand of heaven
seducing her toward what frightened and compelled her.
They watched in disbelief,
bewildered by how quickly
the destruction had started
and how it consumed them.

THE FIGURE

From a blank canvas sprang a swirl of color and emotion:
a mysterious figure emerging from a dark thicket.

Was he beautiful? Did it matter?
For once ugliness could be a form of beauty: an equivalent

to prove the soul's existence.
Dried paint like a second skin on our hands, its oily smell—

was it possible to replicate love?
The paintbrush unleashed a river of blood.

The day darkened in the room. Time lost track.
We forgot our mothers still in bed, the failure of fathers,

secret lives of our sisters. Is it the figure's mystery
that enthralls or the shock of seeing manifest the passion

we longed to hide? Is he our stillborn twin or a lost love
buried under the debris of daily existence? Or the terror

of loss itself? Brutal hands, a slash of red.

On the side of the road a deer, frozen, frigid.
Go back to your life, the voice said.
What is my life? she wondered. For months she lost
herself in work—Freud said work is as important
as love to the soul—and at night she sat with a boy,
forcing him to practice his violin, helping him recite his notes.
Then the ice thawed and the deer came to life.
She saw her jump over the fence, she saw her in the twilight,
how free she looked. She saw her eyes shiny as marbles,
as much a part of this world as the fence a worker
pounds into the earth. At night she still sat with the boy.
He's learning "Au Claire de la Lune."
Do you know it? He has established a relationship
with his violin. He knows that it takes practice to master it:
the accuracy of each note, to wrestle his feelings to the listener.
But he's impatient. Sometimes what he hears and feels
are not always the same. *Again,* the poet says.
She knows if he tries to silence his fervor, he might not ever know
who he is. The poet contemplates whether a deer can dream.
Rich blood-red berries on a branch, pachysandra in the garden.
A soft warm bed in the leaves.

MUSIC IS TIME

Music is time, said the violin master.
You can't miss the stop or you'll miss the train.
One, two, three, four, one, two, three, four,
one, two, three, four.

She clapped her hands together
as the boy moved the bow across the strings.
One, two, three, four, one, two, three, four,
one, two, three, four, the violin master shouted,

louder and more shrill so that her voice
traveled through the house like a metronome,
guiding him, commanding him to translate the beat,
to trust his own internal rhythm.

Good boy, she said.
See how hard you have to be on yourself?
How will your violin know who you are
unless you make it speak?

THE POET CONTEMPLATES THE NATURE
OF MOTHERHOOD

He wants to know his history. It's not enough
to say *I am your mother. Your father is reading
in the bedroom.* He wants to know why
his eyes are blue-gray or sometimes green—
why her eyes are brown. He wants to understand
the lightness of his hair, the sensitivity of his skin,
why music is his language, not theirs.
This is your story, the poet says. *You were born a long time ago.
You were a boy floating in a basket
on the Nile and I was a queen longing for a son
and your father was a king come to claim you
from the water.* No, he says. You're lying. *Why are the leaves
falling? When will it snow? Do you think the boy will find
her again, the woman who cast him out alone?
How did she know he wouldn't drown?
But he's not alone,* she says.

RULES OF CONTACT

A ball is cracked into the air and the underlings
in their red caps field it. A line drive; another

to the boy at third. *Get under it. Don't be afraid.*
Let's hear some chatter. It's late in the day.

Have you noticed that everyone is separating?
a mother from the bleachers remarks, knitting

her anxiety into careful knots. *Where are the sparrows?*
The sun rests over the awning of trees,

wind's compass stopped, gone awry.
One boy refusing to comply steals second.

Is disorder a rally against resignation?
Boys bow their heads beneath the sun's glare.

The boats along the Hudson move in slow motion,
unmoored from the dock.

How to quell the current rising against the boat?
How to trust what moves beneath it?

The Lord of the Field hits a high fly,
in homage to his disciples. *Look alive.*

Get behind the ball. Stay on top of it.
Hurled faster than the speed of light

the ball travels from one boy's mitt
to another boy's in perfect orchestration.

My son won't let me kiss him anymore,
a mother on the bleachers decries.

THE POET CONTEMPLATES HER CALLING

Come to me, he said, *I want to touch you.*
I will never disappear. The voice was deep and resonant
as if it belonged to her true nature. Some nights
enchanted by the voice and its lyric resonance—
the memories it evoked—she could hear nothing else
save its desperate music. *Stay with me,* he said, *don't go back,*
and the divide between the real and invented
grew like a split in a canyon.
She thought the tender dinners, open window
at the table to allow in fresh air,
their private chitchat sealed off
and protected as if underneath glass
inside the insular walls of their home might be enough.
That she could still follow what compelled
through the narrow courtyard down the unsafe, spiral stairs
and into the mysterious garden if she managed
to live with the disturbances, and she continued to travel further,
to seek more, forgetting she could never turn back,
even when the voice grew so faint she could barely hear it,
to ponder what she had left behind.

They peered into the hole in the broken stained glass of the cathedral
and the boy saw that it was a sculptor's studio in the basement

of the grand church, all dust and plaster and half-finished
sculptures in abundance. *I don't feel like myself anymore,* he said.

The boy was eight. He knew how to read, play music, calculate
his times table. He had abandoned one set of heroes for other heroes.

The biblical garden lush with autumn flower, the morning brash,
brilliant, curling itself inside and around the open spaces within

the close, the boy's eyes on fire as he glimpsed an interior world
viewed through a broken window. Through the peephole he watched

the sculptor chisel into the body of the statue; witnessed
the mysterious alignment of faith and vision turned out of stone.

Her face is in pain, he said, unaware of suffering in pursuit of beauty.

MYTH OF CREATION

With nothing but a pencil and a blank sheet
of thin-skinned paper the empire forged itself
without will or reason upon the dreamer,
luring her toward reciprocation until the tip
of her finger formed a callus, until word
by word, sentence by sentence, sense by sensibility
found their own scurrilous logic.
Trust me, said the voice, who seemed to be
a second self, a shadow. *There is no free will
without pain.* A touch against her skin
signified the fragility of being, the elusive trees
were her fathers, books her teachers; her heroes
were statues in the museum garden.
She traveled through the city, its history etched
in the brick of marble buildings;
searched faces for meaning though not one face
struck her alike. *Don't be afraid,*
the voice said, as if fear were another definition for happiness.
And for one moment the world revolved
around her like a sea of shimmering stars
where she was the center of the universe,
where she shut the door and no one dared enter,
where she dreamt of lovers who would never want her,
where the rain fell regardless.

THE POET CONTEMPLATES
THE INTENSITY OF EMOTIONS

Like extreme weather, volatility
has the ability to threaten the stability of any field.
The poet suggested that if she were not moved
when the kindergartners sang "My Country, 'Tis of Thee"
facing the American flag, if the woman on the subway
mumbling to herself did not provoke memories
of lost relatives in war, if snow on the cornices
of the library did not excite her, how could she be expected
to believe in the longevity of passion?
If she did not awaken some snow-swept mornings
restless, filled with a desire she could not name
or replenish, then how would she know
when she was happy? (Did the marriage counselor
really suggest she hide her despair? Aren't secrets forbidden?)
The winter has been cold this year.
When the weather comes on the evening news
there's reason to stay up late. Wind chill. Snow drifts.
Arctic temperatures. Fog against the window.
What does God have in mind, giving us snow again,
when for so many winters we've been deprived?
Snow of our childhoods, snow of our dreams,
snow falling on the train from Moscow
to Saint Petersburg when Vronsky followed Anna,
convinced he could not live without her.

II

INTIMACIES: PORTRAIT OF AN ARTIST

1. The Seeker

Has she nothing else to do
lounging on the bed in midday
while the young artist
perches on a table at the footboard
staring at her naked body?
On the table is a bowl of fruit.
Through the slats in the blinds
light slashes shadows across
the woman's body like wounds.
Held in the sealed envelope
between her crossed legs,
a promise. Her face bears
the look of agony. His of wonder,
of pleasure. Or perhaps she is the seeker
looking inside the boy's eyes
just before he bares himself
so that she might rescue her dignity.
So that he might lose his.

2. Adjoining Rooms

She poses in a room
somber as a still life.
The floor cast in the orange stain
of a pumpkin, the blood orange
of a fruit cut open like a burst
of brightness. No one penetrates.
No one escapes the black-blue walls.
Her hair is long and wavy as a girl's
but gone gray and coarse.
Her naked body lures us closer,
permits us to see too much.
In another room her daughter practices.
In satin bodice and tutu,
in white tights and silk toe shoes,
hair pulled back tightly in a bun.
Her hands reach out into pirouette.
The two faces are the same.
One the hue of the other.
A twin odor reigns.

3. Slumber Party

It is the navy blue light
of a suburban evening when all myths are born.
Through the open windows, through the light from the sky,
the leaves on the branches sparkle.
Twinkle like lights on a party boat.
Two boys inhabit the low alcoves of the hot attic.
Two separate selves existing in one boy's room.
Always one wants to be like the other,
wants to possess him.
(They're not brothers.) Oh, to be the boy
whose back is turned, wearing only his white briefs.
He kneels in front of the TV as if to a savior.
The other boy is exposed, naked.
He enters the open white sheets,
the trundle underneath pulled out in invitation.
On top of the TV an erotic doll
spins, casting shadows in the room.
Will the boys always turn against each other?
Will the doll stop spinning? Will the shadows
of our boyhood selves cease to be?

4. Saturday Night

Don't be afraid. Come closer.
It's bath time. The boy's in the tub,
Father's shaving, Mother is dressed
in her evening wear: black silk slip,
high heels, leaning on the tub's edge.
Listen as she inhales her cigarette.
Listen to the splash. It's intimate. Private.
Feel the humidity rise, hear the slide
of the razor shimmy down Father's neck.
Watch the little boy pee into the water.
Look into Mother's eyes. What truth
do they belie? Is she no longer enchanted?
I know you feel you've intruded
on their privacy, entered their secrets
and lies, invaded their private space.
I know you want to leave. But the boy,
he's you, isn't he? Doesn't he make you ache?

5. Family Vacation

The Ping-Pong table is available.
Do you want to give it a try? To volley with me?
Or perhaps you'd rather watch the nudes.
Look how comfortable they seem sprawled
on their inflatable mattresses in the sand.
The little girl with her long pigtails,
she's old enough to be his daughter.
The middle-aged women in their string bikinis
walking the beach, the feckless teenage boys
sparring with their rackets, the woman reaching
for higher volume on the boom box,
the one-armed man, what casualty befalls him?
It's tropical here. Take my hand.
You're getting too much sun.
The dog of some uncertain pedigree
digs his paws into the sand.
It's uncomfortable this time of day.
No shade. No trees save those palms
in the distance. Watch out. Shield yourself.
He's ready to run.

III

IN CONTEMPLATION OF THE HUSBAND

Suitors lured her away
with promises of secrets and abandon.

She was a locked door
without a key, a house without windows

to peer in, or perhaps he neglected
to seek her out.

His razor and comb gather dust.
The coins in his drawer are tarnished.

Private disquisitions, mysterious glances,
blood and grief woven into the epic of cloth

too precious to unravel.
Sometimes in moonlight's disguise

she thinks she sees him peering into the garden.
Rich forest and burn of wind on his skin,

voiceless wonder of her dreams,
recanting the nature of their attraction.

In proof of her theorem he strings his bow
and shoots a piercing arrow.

By dawn it is all erased.

ANNIVERSARY

The bouquet was on the table.
It was a bouquet of fall flowers,
daylilies and red chokeberries,
gold daisies and purple hibiscus,
too robust for the vase to contain.
She had consulted with the florist.
A desire to name each family,
not to forget. *Lady in Waiting:*
a strand, with a chain of little red flowers
and a thick husky stem.
All week the bouquet had dropped petals,
filling the table with debris,
yet still she replenished
the vase with fresh water,
not wanting to let it die.
It was a grand arrangement.
By week's end it began to stink
slightly, that smell of warm, rotting,
humid earth, of something
that had simmered too long,
that needed new air to breathe.
She tried to cut the stems
to preserve them longer.
They were too thick to sever.
She took out the withered stalks,
making room for the flowers that still held on.
Her floor was a mess
of broken stamens and pollen.
Her sink was all petals,
where they'd bled.
There was more life left. *Not yet.*
No.

INTRUDER

He was quiet.
He wasn't speaking.
He was quiet unto himself.
That's what she liked about him,
how he took her to lost places
and uncovered secrets inside her
she longed to disclose.
How his presence gave her the will to do so.
How his quiet hunkered inside him
like a baby curled in a woman's womb,
and when it was finally pushed out, there was a flood,
a torrential outpouring of mucus and blood
and then this live thing kicking, crying, screaming,
demanding she pay attention. And then once she did
he was gone again, curled up, fast asleep,
sucking his thumb.

She drove through the park and noticed
the leaves had almost changed completely.
Where had she been?
The trees were red, orange, yellow,
leaves falling everywhere when before
it had been green, tame, lush.
How close she was to missing it.
The sun pressed up against the passenger window.
She was the passenger.
She longed to stop time.
Hold the trees. Stop the leaves from turning.
Get her hands dirty.

The intruder turned his head toward hers.
He kissed her. He traced her face
with his hands.
He had no name, no shape,
no voice, no familiarity with anyone she knew.
She had to face the fact that he was in her dreams,
beckoning her to follow.

She had to face the fact
that the leaves were turning, fading,
before she could rejoice in their demise,
that it made her crazy
how red and brilliant they became
before they died, how she wanted them to keep
changing, or not.
How she wanted to stop.
How she didn't want to change
and not know who she was
and whether she even liked the intruder
dressed in his cloak of many colors.

SUBTERFUGE

What are the rules? she said,
apprehensive, longing not only
for the rain to stop
(suddenly it built in force)
but to look out for the two yellow birds
that skirted through the field
the morning before, weaving their way
through the flurry of the yard,
excited by their own dare.
You know the rules, he said.
There are boundaries.
The field of wild brush
separated one house from the other.
Even when it was quiet
you sometimes heard the child
screaming with laughter in the yard,
could intuit the mood of the house
and its inhabitants, share in their intimacy.
The rain turned to storm. It pushed
against the windows, threatened to seep
into the cracks underneath the windowsill.
It slashed against the shingles, as if the house
were a boat and subject to the tide of water.
In the wind's determination was a force
that wanted to carry you with it,
engulf you in its madness
and then throw you spent into the field,
sure of itself and its need to purge and punish.

THE END OF LOVE

She was in her kitchen,
with the cool blue impenetrable quiet
she had craved and she remembered
the excursion of his warm hand
on her skin, the idea of a family
he had embodied, the strength
of his love for her still intact,
like a city underneath the earth
that had failed to fully prosper.
She remembered the day they had met
when they were young and different,
and she probed that moment
as she did all things until she was exhausted
by the what-if and whatnots and what would come to pass.
She saw her entire life pass
into all the objects in the house,
and she was reminded
of the familiarity of a full life as she had lived it:
the symmetry of color, of shapes so perfect
you didn't want to touch or disrupt
the arrangement; the orchestration of their bodies;
how they had grieved,
the quiet distillation of his essence,
filling her house with breaths
so unlike her own.
When it happened, it came as something inevitable,
without expectation, without notice,
with a life and force of its own,
changing everything, even the quality
of air they had grown to depend on,
and they hadn't known how to stop it,
and then she knew it wasn't the end,
it was only the beginning.

IV

THE SKIERS

I

It begins with snow. The lone wilderness.
An intruder, high in the silver hill-
top. A racer, he swiftly glides the slick
mountain back, slips between startled lovers—
no forewarning. He leaves a trail of Ss
in his track. Breathless, he lies in the snow
beside the frozen wonder of the lake,
stirred by the intimacy of lovers.
How long since he tasted the bittersweet
sap running through the maple's heart, or stopped
to listen to the language of the lark?
All the young squires in their down jackets
and stocking caps surround him. *Follow me,
Pandemonium* high on the crescent.

II

She thought it was a dream. She couldn't breathe.
The voice was in her head, inside the clat-
ter. It stole from her. She couldn't see. Snow
kicked up. A blizzard of emotion in
its wake a blur of black—the terror of
happiness rushed past. He whispered that she
was beautiful. A lark. She looked ahead.
She tried not to listen. It was as if
in that glance she saw her entire life
pass: passions set awhirl in blinding am-
bition. Who would she be if she turned back?
The cold hurt. A branch fell. She followed the
loops of her betrothed's trustworthy path, a-
gainst fierce wind and gradient's resistance.

III

The racer scans the enormous valley.
It's all snow, a field, a paradise of
white. Lovers locked in an embrace against
an evergreen tall and grand, its branches
appear to yield seeds of awareness. Her
face like a jewel, too bright to steal. He stops
at the ledge above the Great Divide to
navigate his path, springs forward and sails
again between them. She loses footing,
tumbles. Is it a dream, that voice she hears
as he dangerously whisks past? The guard
calls out in warning. Clouds disperse behind
firs and tall cedars. A black-tailed magpie
cries. The racer is banished from the slant.

IV

The wind changes direction. Rushing through
steeples of evergreens, spruces, sighing,
moaning, causing fragile branches to creak,
turning ground asunder. Where is the new
snow? The slope is rock, patches of broken
ice, clumps of trodden grass. The imprint of
a body fallen from the cliff. Injured
wings braided in snowy patterns. How bit-
ter, wind. How cruel. Underneath an over-
pass a divide of water. Evergreens
crowned with tinsel. Beneath the frozen lake,
schools of hungry fish. Ashes shiver. Is
there any light left in the cold mountain's
interior? The wind does not subside.

V

Or is it simply the sun's shadow spread
over the valley toward the village to
tell the rest of mankind the intruder
is not alone? *Don't follow,* the shadow
seems to say. It is treacherous, the moun-
tain air, the elevation, dips and gaps.
Don't be tempted. The dark unreasoned path
and miles of vacant powder camouflage
the lack of undergrowth. Two bald eagles
mated for life unless one dies leave their
sturdy treetop nest made of scraps of twigs,
soft moss, feathers to scrounge for the remains
of the bodies of the weak and lost who
did not survive their desperate hunger.

VI

Suspended over the sunken valley
from the lower bowl to Earth, the racer
traverses into winter garden. Dead-
fall, unforeseen rocks and boulders. The wind
is forbidding. An avalanche set loose
in the path. All a blur. A mirage of
white. She cannot see beyond the madness
of evergreens where not even a hawk
has trespassed. He falls with her. And as they
fall is aroused to love her. In fury,
unsure of fate, as if they are still a-
lone, desperate to circumvent the past,
they bed in a froth of wet leaves against
the eerie echo. The terrain is marked.

VII

Who is to judge the argument? The sky's
fury. Where is the red-tailed hawk, the scrub
jays, magpies, ravens? Is there no spark left
in the mountain's core? Can no living thing
survive without passion? The skiers are
alone, naked and spent amidst the grand
peaks. She cannot breathe. The mountain air ex-
hausts her. Was it all a dream? Bright powder,
voice in the wind, swiftness of its power
to transfigure. Leaves fix to her cold skin.
The dark gem of the heart a conundrum.
Descending gracefully down the slope, comes
the banisher of the interior,
offering warm blankets of devotion.

VIII

There is a tear in the dark sky. No light.
The slopes are cold, barren. The lone racer
traverses the mystique of the Great High-
way called Chaos where only daredevils
have crossed. He has fallen off the slope, his
skis no longer seduce the bare mountain.
He is alone, besieged by the shadow
of the peaks. The sun has scourged the slope, un-
burying patches of scruff and mud, a lost
scarf, a necklace of tinsel. Dwarfed ever-
greens litter the path. Gone is the blind pu-
rity, the sparkle. The earth's exposed to
its fundamental state without the van-
ity of beauty to obscure its fate.

IX

The mountain is forever divided.
The back bowl and the forward. The quarrel
in the wind does not subside as if caught
in a vortex forever in mourning
for the unchangeable past and yearning
to break free of its stronghold. *Who am I?*
Night's owl calls. Snow accumulates. It can-
not stop. The earth tastes its sweetness. The side
of the mountain is spare, free of tree and
vegetation. Dark, unseasoned, as if
there's a breach in the mountain's heart. Where are
the hummingbirds, jays, and falcons? Once wild-
flowers dotted the bluff. Bald eagles soared
over aspen. Now mist obscures the view.

X

Across the peak the shadow of a deer
and her hart neither frivolous nor star-
struck and her slender, spotted, just-born fawn,
legs still twisted from the womb, tucked behind
and licked almost clean of its smell to pro-
tect from harm as if to remind of the
possibility of love. Once two bucks
in agony fought to claim her scent. Un-
furled by the ferocious wind, aroused, snow
blows in circles, exposing what it meant
to conceal. One version of paradise:
Artemis, goddess of fertility
and the hunt transformed into a stag. For
one moment the world is perfectly calm.

THE POET CONTEMPLATES THE SUNFLOWERS

This is how she imagines it. A stillness.
He enters the room and is not afraid.
Once the poet watched a fence being torn down
picket by picket. It was white and surrounded a garden.
Inside the garden was a bed of sunflowers.
The toughest flower. She cut their stems
to put in a tall vase on her table
and it was as if she were cutting through a cord.
The poet likes sunflowers in the garden
where they are a part of the earth.
It was a mistake to have taken them indoors.
The black center face-to-face with her
at the table, stems almost as tall,
the crown of yellow petals.
It was a mistake to take something from the soil
in which it grows and try to separate it
from the kingdom of its parenthood.
They knew each other a long time ago.
They were twins in another life.
A psychic who lived in the back apartment
read her cards when she was young and afraid.
Nightly the poet watched the psychic's clients trail in
eager for news. *Will my daughter get married?*
Will the baby survive? Does he love me?
Who am I? What do you see?
The poet can see things he doesn't want her to see.
She knows what his body feels like and they have never touched.
She knows that when he says he can't see her
it is because she is all he sees.
She knows when he says *don't,* it means *please.*
She doesn't know why she has designated him as the keeper—
it's not rational—as if only he held the key
and once unlocked, what?

THE POET DISCOVERS THE SIGNIFICANCE
OF THE OLD MANUSCRIPTS

It was a book as complex and profound as an epic masterpiece.
A book filled with pathos and history. A book about writing
brushes and inkstones. A book of betrayal and lust and madness.
A book that wanted to devour its reader with desire.
"Its innards were once fiery hot," the book said.
It had survived hundreds of years. They were at the Morgan
looking at the lost manuscripts of erotic poems under glass.
The poet thought of all the colors of pain
and suffering, not to mention the joy it required
to make one single line of verse. Or fiction.
She sat on a bench afterward drinking cold bad coffee
and denouncing the chapter on passion. "Press down on the hairs.
Let the writing brush . . ." There was no sun. It was a gray morning
and her small feet were frozen in her open-toed sandals.
She would forgo the book of songs; she would forgo
the book of laughter; she would forgo the book of acquisitions.
She would forgo the book that held no other equivalent
in life save the rush of pure feeling dripping like ink
from a pen. She had read that according to Daoist
medical theory the body contains in microcosm
the essential force of the universe, or chi, which is made up
of the male principle, yang, and the female principle, yin.
Each wanted to imbibe the other's life force.
She was free to write her own discourse.
All those colors flooding her, moving inside her.
All those words. They were rushing from her pen.
Making strange loops on her paper.
They'd been drinking, it was a long night of drinking
that frightened her.
They'd made it up her stairs and into the small room
the size of a closet. He was so tall he had to slump a little
and when she looked up at him it was like looking up the lean walls

of a building. *Please,* she said. *I'm here,* he said.
It was hundreds of years ago.
It was during the days of poems written about sheaths,
days of unwrapping long beautiful robes. Days of prose poems
and lotus flowers. *That perfume. Did you put it on for me?*
And then in the daylight, out in the open, where they'd gathered
to conduct a business of lies and forgo the book of knowledge,
forgo the book with no name, forgo the book of nights
and reminiscences and the book of declarations,
he cut her with a knife.
She was bleeding a blood with no color.
A blood no one could see or touch.
She looked up at the tall building
and it was made of stone. It was a new day.
The modern windows the color of jade.

Once she was infatuated with a potter.
Late nights she left her dormitory and walked
down the hill in Athens of Ohio in the twilight
to the studio to watch him throw his pots
against the wheel. Muddy water spattered
her face, hair. She wanted to partake in his radiance,
certain that beauty was almost secular, earthly,
something to be held and fondled and hence not one's own.
She saw how sand and silt mixed with water
turned to clay, watched, mesmerized as he spun
the wheel, his palms cupped around the mound to steady it—
the deep absorption in his eye. She watched his fingers
slowly raise the slender waist of the vessel,
watched it collapse and rise again.   .
Now she is back in the small hotel,
tired, filled with desire to create,
but as she travels inside the wilderness,
deeper into her dreams and fantasies
she sees that her body is hers now, and not an object
of devotion. Comprehension came not in thought
but in feeling, in concentration, in being present
to the sound of the rain slipping off the roof, the layers
of passing time, the sighs in the Tuscan garden.

THE BEAUTY OF THE CLEARING

She wanted to run. She experienced
the desire in its opposite form, the beloved
fleeing, and when she witnessed
the impulse in herself she felt like one of the actors
trapped beneath the spotlight of a stage; caught, a fraud.
Once the lights went on, she didn't want to leave
her seat, still held captive inside the drama
though by then the cast had retreated to their private dressing rooms.
Without the stage lights, the furniture looked old and shabby,
the floor dust-ridden, an inner dimness projected
on the lifeless stage. The desire to run
was instinctive—it was like running through a forest
dense and crowded by tall poplars,
she could only go one way, following the path
into the open clearing where she sought succor and sensed relief.
The trees slender and indestructible, the earth soft
and pliable beneath her feet. Not a tremble.
She had gone to see the new production
in a mood of disengagement and while
she felt the director had miscast the morphine-
addicted mother she was drawn in nevertheless,
and during intermission, the theater abuzz
with the play's tension, she was moved
to find that an audience could be persuaded,
that the play—*Long Day's Journey into Night*—
had not seemed dated. A man behind her whispered
that the "whole fricking family was codependent"
and at the drinking fountain a young woman
said in O'Neill's hands all relationships are dangerous.
There was one point in the play, Act 4, where she wanted
to jump from her seat and command poor Jamie, the sad, misbegotten

brother (the poet, for God's sake), to leave, flee.
She still waited, hopefully—as if she expected
the characters to change—for the burden to lift,
though she had seen the play before
and knew the inevitable ending.
The true story is this: the beloved
simply wanted to hold her.
The beauty of the clearing, other than the warmth of the sun,
was its steady ground and lack of agitation
(the birds preferred the denseness of the wood).
There were two kinds of light—
light that kissed the tops of the trees
and hence the branches bent
toward it, and light that was destructive,
that absorbed the leaves, taking
a piece of their pigment—and she had never known
how to distinguish the two; better to find
solace in the shade. But it was something else.
When she reached the clearing she lay down
on the grass. The sun was shining.
She discovered it was in the ring of sun
where she longed to be,
it was like being reborn. The ability to hear
and see and feel without fearing
she was depriving someone else
of happiness. And in the clearing she understood
this was happiness.

THE POET RETURNS HOME FOR THE HOLIDAYS

Even the boy said the city was small,
no skyscrapers, crowds of people. Streets a-
dorned with ornaments, Nativity scenes
to please the passersby, the simple life:
hockey games, lunch at the skating club, whole
days reading the papers. The libraries.
So many memories unleashed like bats
escaping from the light in the attic.
When she read her poems at the bookstore near
the square to friends and neighbors with good true
hearts, she wondered what they thought, how she looked
beneath the surface, the place no one wants
to go where trees are fragile, damaged—
the streets entire avenues of loss.

THE DREAM

She was walking away from the house,
down the winding road, farther into the field
past where the horses grazed, through the straight
rows of the grape orchard, beyond the peasant farm
until she could no longer see the roof, the deck, the fence.
Could no longer hear the shots from the hunter.
She felt no attachment to the sky and its incandescence,
no attraction to the shifting of the earth
and its unseasonable cracks, no affiliation
with the cardinals or the scavengers.
All of it was gone—all meaning
she had attached to the significance of life.
She looked at her hands and did not
know them. She touched her face
and felt nothing. Not even want.
She looked at her body and was unclothed;
no one could find or see her.
She walked without destination
or distinction no longer understanding
who she was or where she was going
or whether she had ever understood
the meaning of cherishment.
Time past and time present and time future
had distilled into the oblivion
she once understood as sky.
She kept walking unsure why
she had wanted to be free.

VI

LINKED BY PREVERBAL FEELINGS

A mother and child.

A father and child.

A child and her siblings.

The soul in the presence of God.

The self seeking to form an identity.

The flower appearing in the earth.

The child drawing the flower.

The flower flourishing.

The flower losing sustenance.

The child mourning the sound

of petals falling to the earth.

THE POET CONFRONTS THE SELF

She took off his coat of envy.
She took off his sweater of anger.
She took off his shirt of resentment.
She unclothed the beauty of his torso,
cast free his cloth of pride, unpeeled
his mask of vanity, unadorned his ambition.
She released the falseness from his heavy shoes,
the want that bored a hole in his flagrant heart.
She unbuttoned his pain.
They were in the woods,
having detoured from the path,
luxuriating in the sounds of forest life,
the various and variant calls of birds,
trenchant, deliberate, delighting
in their laughter.
Is this who I am? he said,
naked of the wounds
of his multifarious nature.

DREAMING OF TWO WORLDS
COEXISTING IN HARMONY

Odysseus lived with Calypso on the island.
She did not want to let him go. He drank nectar and ambrosia,
slept in a cave next to a nymph who wanted to make him immortal,
but each day he sat on the same rock gazing out at the sea
weeping for home and Penelope. Back home Penelope waited.
She was like a lighthouse, reigning over the seas, calling him home.
Outside on the deck the poet read about ancient wars and vendettas,
about a son protecting his mother from the dangers of her suitors.
Inside the Knicks were on and she could hear the cheers
and cursing through the screen. On the lawn were two birds,
one pursuing the other, darting through the trees,
creating cacophony and havoc. The long stems of the cosmos
bent in the wind, and then a sound as primal as a first cry
called over the mist, the screen door slammed shut,
and across the field she saw the little one sneak away next door
to fight another war on Nintendo.

AN ESSAY IN TWO VOICES

I

Imagination transfigures the image of the loved one.
The process of falling in love, Stendhal wants to persuade us,
is a process of crystallization. Perhaps you fancy lying in an orchard
looking up at the sky through the branches, how pleasant it would be
to be there with your new acquaintance. She is someone
who would share your feelings for the orchard and the sky.

But suppose now, as is highly probable, you meet
with "some coolness or slight rebuff" on the part of the person
with whom you are falling in love. Whatever the original hopes,
doubt gains a place in your feelings. Perhaps the other
is indifferent; perhaps the initial hopes were misplaced.
Perhaps under the transforming powers
of imagination, there's evidence of a positive attitude toward you.
This is what Stendhal thinks of as the "second crystallization";
and it is at this stage, he believes, that love becomes fixed.

II

The lovers are kissing under the glare of traffic lights.
They have walked for hours along the promenade near the park
in serious deliberation. They have been having the same conversation
for a year now. But we *are* in a relationship, she says. *I know,* he says.
What will happen when you leave, she says. *I'll go back to my life.*
What am I? she asks. *You're not my life,* he says.

THE LISTENER

She could see shapes in the distance
and outlines of objects, smell rusted snow
on metal, taste the cold air, but when she listened
she was awakened to all that had been suppressed:
blood-red suicide of a deer against the lights of a car;
black-wet back of the stillborn runt;
hungry cry of someone she had kissed; dark blue
madness of longing, pale sigh of resignation.
She listened to truck and tractor engines.
Sleigh runners squeaking in the snow,
wind in the woods, geese
near the sea, crows picking
the fields clean. She listened
with such passion as if listening were a grieving
for not seeing. Until even desire itself
became a kind of sorrow.

TOUCH-ME-NOTS

She brought a little of the country into the city
in the pots of impatiens she had planted.
The petals white, pure, the opposite of color.
She had transferred the impatiens from the garden,
digging her hands into soil two parts fibrous loam,
one part leaf mold and peat moss and pushing
the roots into the earth. Despite the quality
of the soil—its rich decomposition of life—
still they would not last. The plants were hardy
and tender, with thick stems and dark green leaves,
the seedpods inside waiting to release, the air
awash in pollen. She looked into the flower
as into a pair of beckoning eyes offering
sustenance independent of a body, free floating
and regenerative and wholly belonging
to what was impossible ever to touch.

LIFT YOUR HEAD, SPEAK

Look up and see the brittle far branches
ready to explode their crumpled blossoms.
The bewildered swan suddenly flaps his
melancholy wings so full of feeling
long forgotten. The desire to hold back,
reach for more keeps him circling the near-
frozen deserted lake. Even the half-
rotten ash's uppermost branch threatens
to bloom. How will the thrush meet its richness?
Where will the squirrel feast and burrow?
Will the groundhog yet embrace her shadow?
Oh spring. Oh fever of dark heat. Oh swan.

BASIC HUMAN NEED FORM

(adapted from Henry A. Murray, *Explorations in Personality*)

ABASEMENT. The need to submit passively; to belittle self.

ACHIEVEMENT. To accomplish something difficult; to overcome.

AFFILIATION. To adhere to a friend or group; to affiliate.

AGGRESSION. To overcome opposition forcefully; fight, attack.

AUTONOMY. To be independent and free; to shake off restraint.

COUNTERACTION. To make up for loss by re-striving; get even.

DEFENDANCE. To vindicate the self against criticism or blame.

DEFERENCE. To admire and support, praise, emulate a superior.

DOMINANCE. To control, influence and direct others; dominate.

EXHIBITION. To excite, fascinate, amuse, entertain others.

HARM-AVOIDANCE. To avoid pain, injury, illness and death.

INVIOLACY. To protect the self and one's psychological space.

NURTURANCE. To feed, help, console, protect, nurture another.

ORDER. To achieve organization, order among things and ideas.

PLAY. To act for fun; to seek pleasure for its own sake.

REJECTION. To exclude, banish, jilt or expel another person.

SENTIENCE. To seek sensuous, creature-comfort experiences.

SHAME-AVOIDANCE. To avoid humiliation and embarrassment.

SUCCORANCE. To be taken care of; to be loved and succored.

UNDERSTANDING. To know answers; to know the hows and whys.

SNOW IN APRIL

It was snowing when I remembered faith—

I always prayed for it when it seemed that prayer was all I could do.

The snow was fine. It misted over the stark trees and formed a layer

over the things I care for, the shapes of buildings, the windows,

the little bushes along the library. The snow reminds me

there is another world I have forgotten because I always forget

how much I love the snow until the air begins to smell of it,

until the sky impregnates and then succumbs.

I had lunch with a friend who reminded me of my sister.

She died in April—the cruelest month (just last week we were touched

by a warm spell and the crocuses had the audacity to show themselves).

I saw in my friend the torment one sees in those who have the need

to understand, to discover, to know, to transcend

the landlocked self. She was beautiful, with her black hair

(though my sister's hair was blonde) and the little wrinkles that formed between her eyebrows when she was thinking hard.

And all along I thought we had to be together to be in love.

I thought we had to share the same roof,

the same child, the same bed.

THE SURFERS

Look how beautiful they are in the distance
Sliding on their boards as they embark
Into the white swirl and cascade
Back and forward. They always take
One step back before they move ahead
On the wave's long journey.

Follow me. Get on your board. Journey
To the breakers in the distance.
I know you're afraid to embark,
To ride the dangerous wave and cascade.
The crest of the breaking pocket takes
the body into the swell ahead.

You're thirsty. All of us are. Ahead
The beach is still. Seagulls mock the journey.
Once we took a fall and lost our way in the distance.
The ocean pulled us under and we embarked
Into the lure of the known and cascaded
Beyond our depth. The sea is not afraid to take

The restless. Or those who forget to take
Caution. The swell is deceptive, look ahead.
Face what threatens to destroy the journey.
Remember one surfer's funeral in the distance
Of memory's long shore? We embarked
On a procession to honor one boy who cascaded

To his death. He rode the cascade
From boy to man in one day. The waves take
Regardless. Is it worth losing what lies ahead?
But if the surfer refuses the journey
How can the wave close the distance?
There's no way back except to embark

Forward. What use is there to embark
Upon the crest of the unknown cascade
If not to enter a new precipice? Take
My hand. No one knows what lies ahead.
Or how to steer the journey.
I know you're tired. I sense the distance

Between us, the vast cascade, the resistance
To embark. The distance ahead.
Take heart. There's meaning in the journey.

THE DREAM LIFE OF THE POET

Everything passes, said her friend, and she waited for it to lift
like fog on the winter beach, bringing clarity—.
She could barely make out the seagulls pecking the sand for crabs,
though she heard their horrible squalls, nor could she see
beyond the turbulence, past the crashing waves into the calmness
of the water. She had always longed for the sea, the way one yearns
for a different life, the dream life
not filled with down-to-earth demands
(she forgot to pick up the dry cleaning),
so that when the actor appeared, reckless, without responsibility,
stepping off one stage into another, she was inside this quandary,
and imagined a life they might have together.
It was a game she played with herself, knowing that he was an actor,
and the world of the stage took precedence.
I want it all, he had said, in a way that seemed seductive.
They were sitting on a bench, lunch hour in the park,
and he confessed he had never allowed himself really to fall.
She took it in the way she took in all things sensual.
It was April, the air still frigid, but she felt the warmth
in the breeze at her cheek and she leaned
toward it, moving her body so that she faced the sun.
In dreams begin responsibilities. She was afraid
to say it aloud, to break the spell. It had been a long winter.
She had attended a show at the Whitney
and was repulsed and provoked by the inflated, comical breasts
John Currin painted on his women, and the strange, twisted, bearded
men—caricatures, she thought, though as the show progressed,

the two naked fishermen at sea,
its nod to Winslow Homer, and "The Lobster" still life,
she understood Currin's grotesque figures were a reaction,
that everything is a reaction to something else.
She stared at the actor. He was good to look at, and in another life
she might have wanted to look longer. *Why do you like to act?*
He stopped picking the paint off the bench with his nail and checking
the coded message on his cell phone. *Because I'm not me.*
The sun fled to the other side of the park
leaving the bench desolate. It was too cold to be outside
and she had never been much of an actress.

Notes

"Intimacies: Portrait of an Artist" is inspired by the following paintings by Eric Fischl: *Bad Boy*, 1981, *Bayonne*, 1985, *Saturday Night: (The Aftermath Bath)*, 1980, and *Saigon Minnesota*, 1985.

"An Essay in Two Voices" is a response to Stendhal's "Love" and his interpretation of falling in love as a process he terms "crystallization." The first section of the poem is an attempt to paraphrase a small part of his argument.

The following fragments from "The Poet Discovers the Significance of the Old Manuscripts" are taken from two poems in *Chinese Erotic Poems*, translated and edited by Tony Barnstone and Chou Ping (Everyman's Library Pocket Poets): "Its innards were once fiery hot," from "A Poem About a Broken Copper Flat-Iron," and "Press down on the hairs. / Let the writing brush . . . ," from "A Poem About Writing Brushes and Inkstones."

The line "Time past and time present and time future" in "The Dream" is derived from T. S. Eliot's lines "Time present and time past / Are both perhaps present in time future," from "Burnt Norton" in *Four Quartets*.

Notes

"Intimacies: Portrait of an Artist" is inspired by the following paintings by Eric Fischl: *Bad Boy,* 1981, *Bayonne,* 1985, *Saturday Night: (The Aftermath Bath),* 1980, and *Saigon Minnesota,* 1985.

"An Essay in Two Voices" is a response to Stendhal's "Love" and his interpretation of falling in love as a process he terms "crystallization." The first section of the poem is an attempt to paraphrase a small part of his argument.

The following fragments from "The Poet Discovers the Significance of the Old Manuscripts" are taken from two poems in *Chinese Erotic Poems,* translated and edited by Tony Barnstone and Chou Ping (Everyman's Library Pocket Poets): "Its innards were once fiery hot," from "A Poem About a Broken Copper Flat-Iron," and "Press down on the hairs. / Let the writing brush . . . ," from "A Poem About Writing Brushes and Inkstones."

The line "Time past and time present and time future" in "The Dream" is derived from T. S. Eliot's lines "Time present and time past / Are both perhaps present in time future," from "Burnt Norton" in *Four Quartets.*

"Lift Your Head, Speak" was inspired by "Emmonsails Heath in Winter" by John Clare, from which I have borrowed two small phrases: "flaps his melancholy wings" and "half-rotten ash."

"Basic Human Need Form" is a found poem taken from Henry A. Murray's *Explorations in Personality* and adapted by Dr. Edwin Shneidman.

Acknowledgments

Grateful acknowledgment to the editors of the following publications in which these poems, sometimes in different forms, originally appeared:

Harvard Review: "Rules of Contact," "An Essay in Two Voices"
The Atlantic Monthly: "Music Is Time"
Open City: "Demon Lover," "Subterfuge"
Kenyon Review: "The Seduction," "The Poet Contemplates the Nature of Reality," "The Poet Contemplates the Intensity of Emotions," "The End of Love," "The Skiers"
The Gettysburg Review: "The Figure," "In Contemplation of the Husband," "The Poet Contemplates the Self."
Cortland Review: "The Poet Contemplates Her Calling"
TriQuarterly: "Intimacies: Portrait of an Artist"
Pequod: "The Poet Contemplates the Sunflowers," "The Beauty of the Clearing," "The Dream Life of the Poet"
Good Roots: Writers Reflect on Growing Up in Ohio, Edited by Lisa Watts, Ohio University Press: "The Poet Returns Home for the Holidays"
Salt: "Snow in April"

I owe a great debt to Eavan Boland, David Baker, and Catherine Barnett for their insightful readings throughout the evolution of this work. I am indebted to Nancy Palmquist for her careful proofreading and counsel. Thanks, as ever, to Deborah Garrison, Jin Auh, and Sarah Chalfant.

Jill Bialosky was born in Cleveland, Ohio. She studied at Ohio University and received an M.A. in Writing Seminars at Johns Hopkins University, and an M.F.A. from the University of Iowa. She is the author of the poetry collections *The End of Desire* and *Subterranean,* a finalist for the James Laughlin Award from the Academy of American Poets. Her poems and essays have appeared in journals such as *Paris Review, American Poetry Review, Kenyon Review* and *The Atlantic Monthly.* She is the author of the novels *House Under Snow* and *The Life Room* and coedited, with Helen Schulman, the anthology *Wanting a Child.* Bialosky is an editor at W. W. Norton & Company and lives in New York City.

A NOTE ON THE TYPE

This book was set in a version of the well-known Monotype face Bembo. This letter was cut by Francesco Griffo for the celebrated Venetian printer Aldus Manutius and first used in Pietro Cardinal Bembo's *De Aetna* of 1495.

The companion italic is an adaptation of the chancery script type designed by the calligrapher and printer Lodovico degli Arrighi.

Composed by Creative Graphics,
Allentown, Pennsylvania

Printed and bound by Thompson-Shore,
Dexter, Michigan

Designed by Soonyoung Kwon